✚ Dad Jokes

For Those Who *SHRED*

Jokes so bad they'll make your family's ski or snowboard day a little better

Brooke Drozdowicz

About This Book

Get ready for over 150 hill-arious, groan-worthy dad jokes for parents, parents-to-be, instructors, coaches, and kids of ALL ages. Keep this in your back pocket for the drive, the shuttle, the lift, the lodge, and sweet, glorious bedtime. Now buckle up and click in because it's all downhill from here.

Acknowledgments

Special thanks to my family and friends who helped teach my kids to shred and to love winter. Thanks for always hanging out with my babies so I could ski, lending handwarmers, wiping boogies, bringing extra candy, picking up skis after a wipeout, and playing endless chairlift games. I wouldn't have made it without you.

Extra special thanks to my husband Brian and our children: Sawyer, Tuck, and Winnie, for sharing some of the best days ever with me on the slopes. I love you lots!

Why was the elephant so good at the halfpipe?

It stomped all the landings

What do you call an albino camel on a ski mountain?

Camel-flage

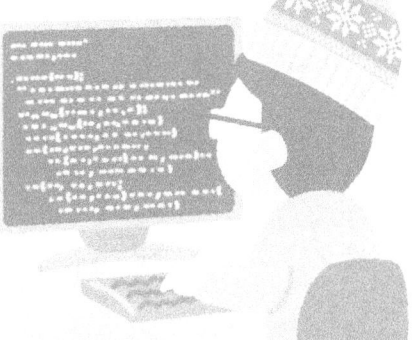

Why do computer programmers make safe skiers?

They "Know the Code"

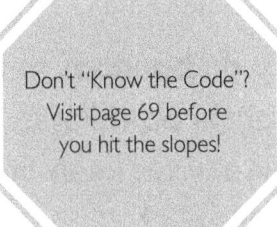

Don't "Know the Code"?
Visit page 69 before
you hit the slopes!

Why did the snowboard instructor get fired?
They swept all their problems under the
magic carpet

What runs all day but never snowboards?
Your nose

**Why do bananas make
great ski patrollers?**
They always keep their
eyes peeled

Knock, knock
Who's there?
Value
Value who?
Value you ski in Transylvania with me?

Knock, knock
Who's there?
Noah
Noah who?
No-ah skiing or riding without a helmet

Knock, knock
Who's there?
Orange
Orange who?
Orange you going to try the mogul trail?

How does a snowboard instructor get to work?
Bi-icicles

What does a Sno-Cat™ eat for breakfast?
Mice Krispies

Who won the rope tow race?
Nobody. It always ends in a tie.

What was the ski tuner's favorite game?
High DIN™ seek

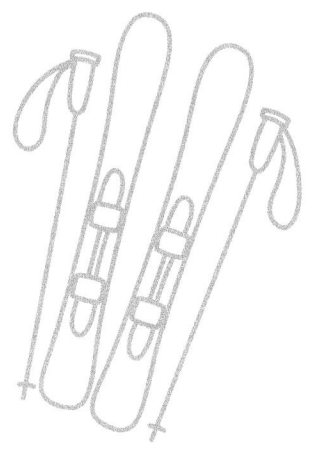

What does a yeti get in their hot chocolate?
Whipped scream

Why did the hair dresser win the snowboard race?
They took a shortcut

How did the ginger-ale snowboard so fast?
Fizz-ics

What do you call the bear ski team?
The Fast and the Furriest

**What is the fish's job at the
ski resort?**
It's a ski tuna

Why did the skier go to the furniture sale?
They didn't want to miss the last chair

What did the Sno-Cat™ order to drink at the lodge?
Meow-ntain Dew

What do you call a skeleton when it forgets its helmet?
A numb-skull

Knock, knock
Who's there?
Witches
Witches who?
Witches the way to the base area?

Knock, knock
Who's there?
Irish
Irish who?
Irish you a fresh corduroy morning

Knock, knock
Who's there?
Howell
Howell who?
Howell you get that ski pole back that you dropped under the lift?

What is the horse's favorite game at the mountain?
Ski-pole-o

How did Venus and Mars know what lift to start at?
They had to plan-et

What did the cat say to their boss when they took a powder day?
The meow-tains are calling, and I must go

What do monsters wear on their feet when they snowboard?
Snowboard BOO-ts

What is a skier's favorite pet?
A Sno-Cat™

Why was the bat so good in the halfpipe?
It was an acro-bat

What did the teenage ripper put on their cheese shop application?
Expert shredder

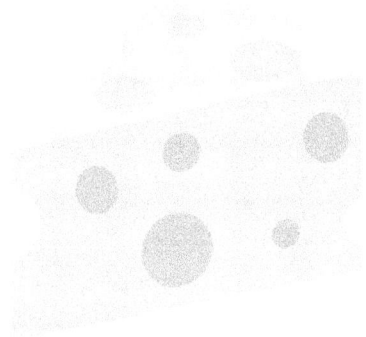

What was the eagle's favorite Olympic event?
Aerie-als

What goes oom-oom?
A cow snowboarding backwards

Knock, knock

Who's there?

Whale

Whale who?

Whale you try to make last chair with me?

Knock, knock

Who's there?

Icy

Icy who?

Icy a little ripper riding a rail

Knock, knock

Who's there?

Ketchup

Ketchup who?

Ketchup to me. If you can!

Why was the possum so good at ski jumping?
It had great hang time

Why are mail carriers great snowboarders?
They always go full send

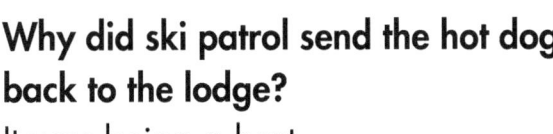

Why did ski patrol send the hot dog back to the lodge?
It was being a brat

Why was the cat disqualified from the giant slalom?

It was a cheetah

What kind of pet did the kid get at their first snowboard lesson?

A magic car-pet

What is a little grom's favorite breakfast?

Frosted Flakes

Why was everyone skiing in a pizza?
It was Pi day

What does the Sno-Cat™ driver say after laying out fresh corduroy?
"Groovy!"

What does the Sno-Cat™ do at the party?
Break the ice

Knock, knock
Who's there?
Heaven
Heaven who?
Heaven seen a double daffy since the 80's

Knock, knock
Who's there?
Ice cream
Ice cream who?
Ice-scream every time I take a double diamond

Knock, knock
Who's there?
Liz
Liz who?
Liz-ten to your instructor if you want to learn to ski or snowboard

Why did the magic carpet operator have no friends?

Everyone just walked all over them

What cereal do they serve in the terrain park?

Trix™

Why did the pancake take a face plant?

It hit flat light

What's a bad golfer but a great skier?
Cheese! It slices in the summer but shreds in the winter.

Why did the cat driver work at the pet salon in the off-season?
They were great at grooming

What happens during bike week at the ski mountain?
You see lots of motor-icicles

How do you keep track of icy spots on the slopes?

A shred-sheet

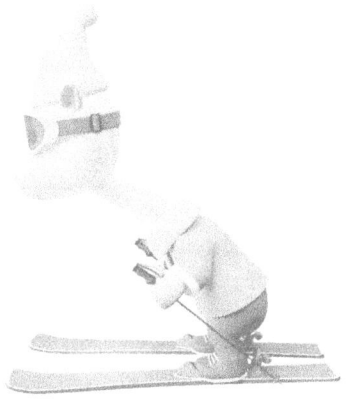

Which giraffe won the giant slalom?

It was a tie, neck and neck to the finish.

What dog breed is the best snowboarder?

A snow-border collie

Knock, knock
Who's there?
Ski
Ski who?
Ski ya later

Knock, knock
Who's there?
Figs
Figs who?
Figs your goggles. You have a gaper gap!

Knock, knock
Who's there?
Olive
Olive who?
Olive a bluebird day

Who took the more difficult trail, the rock or the tree?
The rock. It was boulder.

Why couldn't the snowboarders pick a trail?
They were at a boarder-cross-roads

What was the jelly's favorite event?
The rail jam

Where did the movie star like to ski?

In the celebri-trees

Why did the orange stop halfway down the black diamond?

It ran out of juice

What is a little shredder's favorite subject in school?

Snow and tell

What's a little grom's favorite doughnut?
Powder-ed

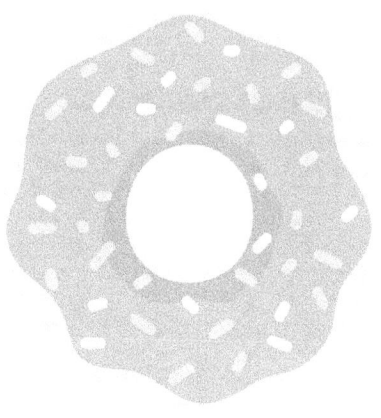

What was the snowboarder's favorite pasta?
Corkscrew

What happened when the bee had to park in the overflow lot?
It had to take the shuttle buzz

Knock, knock

Who's there?

Wool

Wool who?

Wool take a green circle from here

Knock, knock

Who's there?

Abby

Abby who?

Abby snow day to you!

Knock, knock

Who's there?

Snow

Snow who?

Snow one is going to pee their snowsuit today

Why was the egg sore after a long day on the hill?
It hadn't been getting enough eggs-ercise

What do do you call little rippers on a very cold day?
Chilled-ren

Why do computer scientists make great ski racers?
They have great tech-nique

What happened when the pumpkin tried to ski the double black diamond?

It squashed

If you're Russian when you go into the ski lodge and Finnish when you get out, where are you when you're in the ski lodge?

Euro-peein'

Why did the bathtub skip Apres?

It was drained

Why did the chicken get disqualified from the ski race?

Officials suspected fowl play

Where does the beaver suit up for a day on the mountain?

The lodge

When I lost my prescription goggles, guess who I bumped into?

Everyone!

Knock, knock

Who's there?

Bean

Bean who?

Bean a snowboarding instructor isn't easy

Knock, knock

Who's there?

Ida

Ida who?

Ida know how to ski moguls. Do you?

Knock, knock

Who's there?

Wheelbarrow

Wheelbarrow who?

**Wheelbarrow some money
for treats at the lodge**

Where do you learn to shred the gnar?
Board-ing school

What is a police officer's favorite kind of trail?
A cruiser

Why did the snail snowboard so slowly?
It was slug-ish

What item of ski clothing is essential to the giraffe?
A neckwarmer

Why did the kid get referred to an orthodontist?
They had a frontside grind

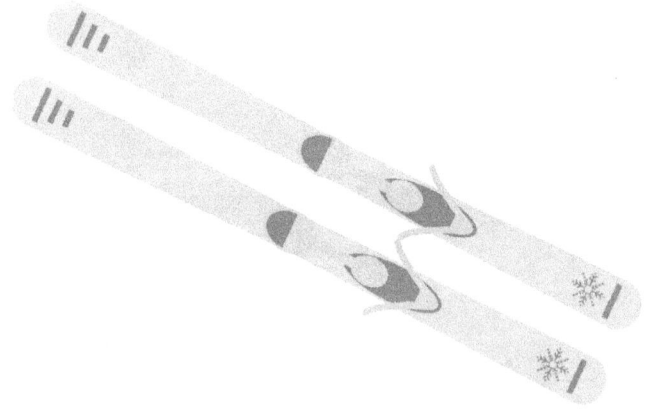

What fish skis on twin tips?
A two-na

Why aren't snowboarders employed as plumbers?

They can only do the half pipe

Which prince ran lessons for first timers?

Aladdin. He took everyone on a magic carpet ride.

What happened when the toothpaste fell in the race?

It was Crest-fallen

Knock, knock
Who's there?
Omelet
Omelet who?
**I can't believe omelet let us go
through the glade**

Knock, knock
Who's there?
Wanda
Wanda who?
Wanda come night skiing with me?

Knock, knock
Who's there?
Avery
Avery who?
Have Avery snowy day

Which tree was the fastest skier?
The al-pine

What did the bee say to the skier that got too close to them?
Buzz off

How does cheddar cheese keep their ski's edges?
Extra sharp

Why did the astronaut dominate the big air competition?
It could really launch

Where did the umpire like to spend time at the mountain?
The base area

What vegetable won the 80's ski weekend race?
The rad-ish

Where does the tortoise snowboard?

The slooooowpe

How did the shampoo get so good at skiing?

Lots of conditioning

Why do some goggles fog up and others don't?

It's a mist-ery

Knock, knock

Who's there?

Honeydew

Honeydew who?

Honey dew you want to take that blue square?

Knock, knock

Who's there?

Kiwi

Kiwi who?

Kiwi try to do french fries instead of pizza on this run?

Knock, knock

Who's there?

Sherwood

Sherwood who?

Sherwood like a powder day

What do you get when your ski instructors are identical?

Twin tips

Which piece of furniture had the longest ski jump?

The couch. It went so-fa.

Why didn't the ski instructor let their students play games in the restroom?

It's not trivial to pee your suit

**What happened to the berries
when the trails merged?**

A traffic jam

What time did the dentist hit the slopes?

Tooth-thirty

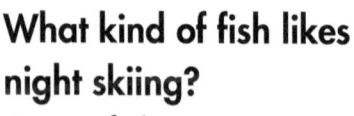

**What kind of fish likes
night skiing?**

A star fish

How did the golfer get up the mountain?

The tee-bar

What does a liftie and the limbo have in common?

They both lower the bar

Knock, knock

Who's there?

Adair

Adair who?

Adair you to hit that kicker

Knock, knock

Who's there?

Snow

Snow who?

Snow use. The peak is closed for avalanche danger.

Knock, knock

Who's there?

Donut

Donut who?

Donut duck the rope or your pass will get clipped

Why did the cheese want to be a liftie?
They liked to string people along

What is a snowboarder's favorite part of the Thanksgiving turkey?
The jib-lets

Why did the tornado win the halfpipe competition?
It could really spin

What kind of cookies do snowboarders hate?
Death cookies

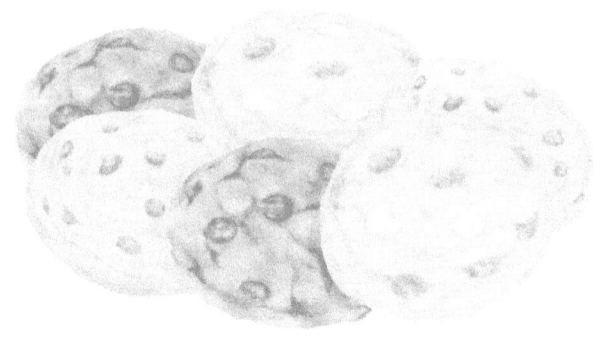

What is a snowboarder's favorite pet?
A snow bunny

Why did the mallard get its pass clipped?
It ducked the rope

What dog breed is the best skier?

An a-ski-ta

Who can ski jump higher than the lodge?

Everyone! Lodges don't jump.

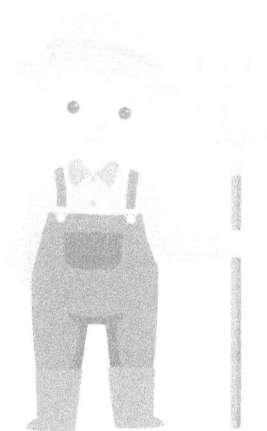

How did the farmer like his slopes in the Spring?

A little corn-y

Knock, knock

Who's there?

Osbourne

Osbourne who?

Osborne to ski! Let's get out there!

Knock, knock

Who's there?

Boo

Boo who?

Don't cry. We can ski again tomorrow.

Knock, knock

Who's there?

Peas

Peas who?

Peas look uphill before pushing off

What happened when the pig took a hard fall?
It pulled a ham-string

How do crocodile parents feed their little shredders after a long day on the mountain?
A croc-pot

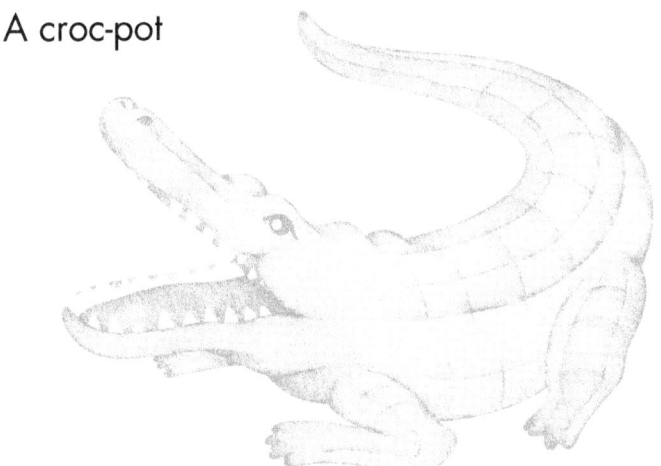

How much does a season pass for a deer cost?
Just a few bucks

Why did the mustang get kicked off the mountain?

Horse-play

What is a parent doing when they're in line and say they ran out of candy?

They're lift lyin'

What is the magic carpet's goal for first timers?

To make them more rug-ged

Why did the cat skin up the mountain?
They didn't want to wait in the lift lion

What did Shakespeare say at the resort's tubing park?
Tube-y or not tube-y

Why did everyone watch the opthamologist at the park?
They were making a spectacle of themself

Knock, knock
Who's there?
Beef
Beef who?
**Beef-ore we get too tired,
we should call it a day**

Knock, knock
Who's there?
Oakham
Oakham who?
Oakham try to get the first chair with me

Knock, knock
Who's there?
Emma
Emma who?
**Emma little cold out here. I should
have worn a balaclava.**

Why did the kid eat a trail map?
Their snowboard instructor said
it would be a piece of cake

What is a skier's favorite dessert?
Ice-crispy treats

**What happened when the whale
tweaked their fin snowboarding?**
They had to visit an orca-pedist

Where did the hen go after night skiing?
Bed! It was eggs-hausted.

Why did the parka agree to take the double black diamond?
It said it was "down" for anything

What was the frog's favorite ski style?
Jump turns

Knock, knock
Who's there?
Lettuce
Lettuce who?
Lettuce ski through the glade!

Knock, knock
Who's there?
Beats
Beats who?
**Beats me. I don't know
which trail they took.**

Knock, knock
Who's there?
Alpaca
Alpaca who?
**Alpaca sandwich in my parka
so I can maximize my vert**

Why did the ski boots fall in love?

They were sole-mates

Customs official: "What is the purpose of your trip?"

Little Grom: "I want to try boarder-cross"

Why did the snowboarder get a job at the coffee shop?

They could really grind

How do frogs clear their goggles?

They use a defrogger

Why did the duck always get first chair?

It got up at the quack of dawn

What was the inventor doing during the blizzard?

Brainstorming

What's a skier's favorite candy?
Ski-ttles

What does a Sno-Cat™ eat for dessert?
Mice-cream

Knock, knock
Who's there?
Iguana
Iguana who?
Iguana learn to ski moguls better

Knock, knock
Who's there?
Lena
Lena who?
Lena little forward to get a better edge

Knock, knock
Who's there?
Yule
Yule who?
Yule never believe how much air I got off that jump

What does the hobo do at the mountain?
They ride the rails

Why did the orca get hired as a snowmaker?
It made killer whale backs

How do you know when there is an elephant in the gondola?
The door won't close

Where does the ski coach hold team meetings?
On Zoom™

Which dairy product won the freestyle competition?
Cheese. It shredded.

Why do sculptors make great snowboarders?
They carve

What do you call frozen boogers?
Snot-cicles

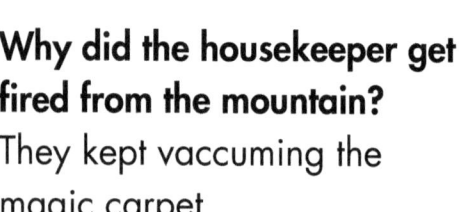

Why did the housekeeper get fired from the mountain?
They kept vaccuming the magic carpet

How do bats navigate moguls?
They use so-gnar

Glossary

Boardercross
snowboarding race where multiple riders simultaneously race down a slope with steep drops and tight turns

Carve
to ski or board such that ski or board edges are driven into the snow to initiate the turn

Corduroy
flat, lined snow surface left after grooming

Corkscrew
off-axis flip that resembles a corkscrew

Corn
snow surface that resembles frozen corn, often occurring during Spring freeze/thaw cycles

Cruiser
well-groomed, smooth trail

Death cookies
hard, baseball to soccer ball-sized ice chunks left by a groomer after a freeze/thaw cycle

DIN™

abbreviation for Deutsches Institut für Normung (German Institute for Standardization). DIN™ setting can be adjusted by a ski technician based on the skier's weight and ability. It determines how easily a skier's boots are released from their bindings.

Duck the rope

accessing a closed trail by skiing or riding under the rope that marks the trail closed. For the safety of yourselves and others, don't do it!

Frontside grind

face forward skiing or riding over anything that isn't snow (i.e. rail, box)

Full send

to approach a trick, jump or slope without hesitation

Gaper gap

the gap on someone's forehead between between their helmet and goggles

Glade

partially cleared forest trail

Gnar

short for gnarly. Refers to challenging terrain and snow conditions.

Grind

skiing or riding over anything that isn't snow (i.e. rail, box)

Grom
young skier or rider

Halfpipe
U shaped snow feature that skiers and boarders perform aerial tricks on

Jib
park feature that isn't made of snow (i.e. rail, box)

Kickers
jump with a curved ramp that allows users to get air

Know the Code
National Ski Areas Association's responsibility code that defines safety guidelines each skier and rider must abide to improve safety on the slopes (see page 68)

Launch
to move up and forward rapidly off a jump

Liftie
nickname for a lift operator

Moguls
mounds of snow that form on ski slopes

Park Ops
the team that creates and maintains park features like rails, boxes, kickers, jumps, etc.

Rails
metal bars, often elevated, that freestyle skiers and boarders slide down

Rail jam
freestyle competition where skiers and riders perform their best tricks on a variety of features (i.e. kickers, boxes, rails)

Shred
to ski aggressively and masterfully

Skins
alpine touring equipment that sticks to the bottom of skis, allowing users to travel uphill without sliding backwards

Sno-Cat™
vehicle that grooms the slopes

T-bar
ski lift in which skiers and boarders lean against a T shaped bar and are pulled up the mountain like a rope tow

Terrain Park
area where a variety of features (i.e. kickers, boxes, rails) are maintained

Twin tips
skis with elevated tips both in the front and the back that allow for skiing backwards

Vert
short for vertical distance

Whalebacks
large piles of snow left by snowmaking equipment before they are groomed out

Do you "Know the Code"?

The National Ski Areas Association developed rules and expectations for skiers and riders in order to promote safety for yourself and others on the slopes. The Code was updated in 2002.
To learn more visit www.nsaa.org

YOUR
RESPONSIBILITY CODE

1 Always stay in control. You must be able to stop or avoid people or objects.

2 People ahead or downhill of you have the right-of-way. You must avoid them.

3 Stop only where you are visible from above and do not restrict traffic.

4 Look uphill and avoid others before starting downhill or entering a trail.

5 You must prevent runaway equipment.

6 Read and obey all signs, warnings and hazard markings.

7 Keep off closed trails and out of closed areas.

8 You must know how and be able to load, ride and unload lifts safely. If you need assistance, ask the lift attendant.

9 Do not use lifts or terrain when impaired by alcohol or drugs.

10 If you are involved in a collision or incident, share your contact information with each other and a ski area employee.

Know and Obey the Code.
It's Your Responsibility.

If you need help understanding the Code, please ask an employee.

Brooke Drozdowicz finally wrote the book she needed when her three children were learning to ski. Attitash is her home mountain and her favorite trail there is Illusion. Nobody cares that she telemarks.

Coming soon!

Dad Jokes
for
Ballers

Jokes so bad they
deserve a penalty

Brooke Drozdowicz